Cryptocurrency King

by Mike Montgomery

Table of Contents

CHAPTER ONE: BASICS OF CRYPTOCURRENCY 3

CHAPTER TWO: MINING 8

CHAPTER THREE: CRYPTO COINS 18

CHAPTER FOUR: BITCOIN SCAMS 30

CHAPTER ONE
BASICS OF CRYPTOCURRENCY

What are cryptocurrencies?

Crypto or digital currencies are only online. They are not issued or supervised by the central bank. Cryptocurrency is paid on the internet, but formally, it is not money. The money that we pay or receive on the internet is like the money we hold in a wallet. It has the same value and name, and it is controlled and regulated by the central bank. Today there are also virtual cryptocurrencies. Bitcoin is one of the most famous cryptocurrencies. Bitcoin is globally accepted for online payments; although it is not issued by the central bank, nor is it linked to accounts with commercial banks. So, it is technically not money.

A cryptocurrency is a form of digital asset that is used as a means of exchange, using cryptography as a way of restricting transaction security, controlling the creation of additional monetary units and confirming currency transfers. Cryptocurrency functions as an electronic record of certain values stored in electronic money on websites that provide such a service. These sites hold the cryptographic in an e-wallet. We charge the wallet by exchanging ordinary money for Bitcoin on the internet stock exchanges. Bitcoin is created by computer processors on computers around the world. In addition to being able to make money by solving complex computer algorithms or "mining," it can also be purchased via Bitcoin ATMs, or online stock exchanges.

Cryptography is a science that deals with methods of preserving the secrecy of information. Information can become vulnerable to interceptor tactics. Such problems can be avoided by encrypting information, which makes it unavailable to interceptors. Code and digital signatures are cryptographic techniques used to implement security measures. The basic element used is called the encryption algorithm, and each system includes a pair of data transformations, called encryption and decryption.

Blockchain technology uses cryptography to link and secure records in "blocks." It has enabled digital information to be distributed, rather than copied, creating the basis for how it stores and transfers data. This technology was created for the needs of the digital currency, but, in the meantime, its enormous potential has become an important topic in many industries, especially the financial sector.

This is especially important when dealing with a huge number of documents and iterations; in the first variant it takes a lot more time and there is a greater the likelihood of error.

Blockchain does not serve to share documentation, but the concept is similar. Time is money. Its value is especially emphasized today when financial transactions in the digital universe are significantly slower than sending email, chatting on any messenger or working on the cloud. Because clients live in this super-fast digital universe, they perceive banks as slow and inefficient, precisely because the speed of transactions can't keep up with the speed of other information they share every day.

However, the position of the banks should also be understood. The priority for the bank is the security of this information, rather than the speed of their exchange. The bank is, traditionally, a place where your money is safe. The moment when security is not a bank's priority it is no longer a bank.

In order to overcome this obstacle, banks are looking for a platform that has the following characteristics:

1. The information moves through a secure network

2. Information must not be manipulated during or after the transaction

3. The transaction information must be delivered to the correct recipient

4. The speed of sharing information to all involved parties must be maximized

5. Settlement must be in real time for all involved parties

Blockchain enters the scene here. The blockchain is based on a distributed database that contains encrypted data that can't be changed or disturbed. It contains two types of data transmission chains. They are transactions and blocks.

Transactions are information, that is, data transmitted. Blocks are part of the chain in a complete process (hence the name of blockchain), which governs the transmission of information. Blocks are interconnected with nodes making such a chain.

Therefore, blockchain can be presented as a distributed, decentralized database, divided into blocks interconnected with nodes, which allows secure transmissions in real time; it does this using mathematical models for distributing encrypted information through a block of blocks. Blockchain transaction participants are connected through knots, and mathematical logic finds free nodes and transmits the transaction from node to node based on the fastest flow in order to pass it to the destination.

In order for financial institutions to use blockchain, it is necessary to provide the following:

1. Each participant in a transaction must be uniquely identified

2. Each participant must be part of an integrated network

3. The participant may be a direct or indirect part of the network

The difference between the existing transaction system is that the transaction is blocked independently.

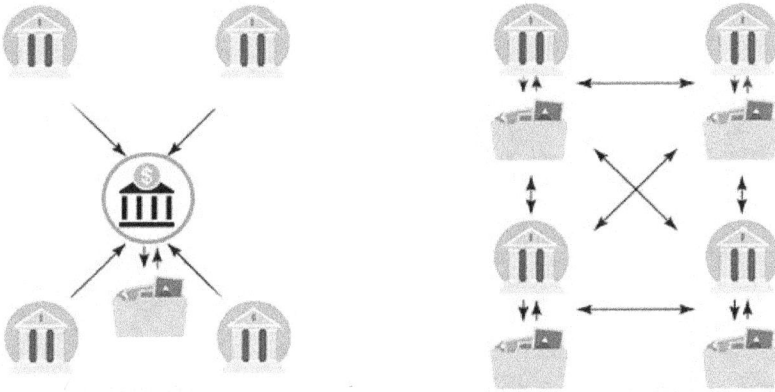

Existing process   Blockchain

A client of bank1 wants to transfer funds from his account to the client's bank account 2. Bank 1 initiates an instruction for transferring money to an account in a bank 2. The mathematical logic of blockchain's instruction creates a transaction and assigns it to the block. The block finds the closest free low-load node and assigns a weight to the path. In the same way, the block will find the next free path, reaching bank 2.

The basic rule for forwarding a transaction through the blockchain is finding the path with the least weight. The sides of a single transaction are linked the entire duration of the transaction. The most efficient path is calculated automatically and in real time, so the total transaction time is measured by microseconds, one-millionth of a second. For this reason, blockchain technology is currently an important topic in financial circles.

MasterCard and Visa cards actively work with developers on this, and both have created APIs for this technology. The moment has never been better for the global business community to take advantage of new payment technologies and upgrade some of the most important processes necessary for their business. Blockchain is developing new solutions to enable our financial sector partners to provide an efficient, transparent way for global money transactions.

CHAPTER TWO
MINING

Types of mining

There are two types of mining:

1. Rig mining, which is additionally divided into pool (group) mining and solo mining

2. Cloud mining

Each of these types, which will be clarified in the text below, use the following process:

The mining computer gets an order to approve a certain set of transactions. Technically, it receives data from the internet in which it is written who sends the smallest number of crypts.
The computer builds a block, a list of transactions to be confirmed. How many transactions will be on the block depends on their size; transactions sent to many addresses are larger than others, as we have explained in this before.

The computer connects all of these data from all transactions (literally pastes them into one whole), and some other data, and then creates the last part of this puzzle - a value that, when added to that set of glued data and the hash, gives a new hash with a certain number of zeros. The number of attempts that can be performed each second depends on the power of a computer.

After the break, the computer that succeeded in the task receives a reward for the block, which currently amounts to 12.5 BTC with Bitcoin mining, or 6.18 XMR if you are mining Monero.

The power of the computer is measured in the number of hits (or hash) per second: H/s (hash/Sec). Depending on the algorithm used, it is often more cost-effective to mine using graphics cards than the processor. So, many buy graphics cards and build mining machines just with them. With a stronger computer, the chance of solving the problem increases.

Many enter mining thinking, "so what if my computer is not be the strongest in the world. Sooner or later I will hit one block and get a reward. Even if this is in 5 years, if I get 12.5 BTC that's over $65,000. It's worth it." This is a mistake not only because in 5 years the prize will not be close to that which is today, but also because many do not realize that mining is like a competitive sport.

When a block confirmation is requested, various miners actually compete.; the goal is to be the first to successfully hit and not run-off. The one who hits the second, third, tenth, etc. does not get anything (except in Ethereum where others sometimes get less Ether as a comforting reward). Therefore, competition with stronger computers makes little sense, especially with the more established and popular crypts like Bitcoin. This problem can be avoided by switching to pool mining, where attempts to strike are sent to the pool of all attempts from all other miners connected to that network. That pool then functions as a solo miner, and after winning the prize, it is divided in fair proportions to all participants depending on who sent the attempted hits.

Bitcoin Pool is a community of Bitcoin miners, who together dig and share Bitcoin earnings. By mining in the pool, you have a constant inflow of Bitcoin, in proportion to your engagement. Within each pool, after logging in, you can assign each mining device as a worker in the mining process, and they become a part of the pool. The pool that operates the operation usually takes 1% of the profit for itself. This slightly reduces the reward for participants, but on average it increases since common power is usually more profitable than private.

The process has the following problems:

If Ethereum switches to the PoS (Proof of Stake) mining system, using powerful computers will no longer make sense. The block award in the Ethereum system is gradually decreasing. Now it's 5. It will soon be 3. Later it will be even less. A 40% reduction is not trivial.

The weight of mining is gradually increasing as the reward decreases - with the goal of switching to the PoS consensus. This means that the machines not only receive fewer rewards but also become less efficient in mining.

Electricity costs and can increase at any moment, thus moving profit margins in an unfavorable direction. How many times have you experienced a decrease in electricity prices? And how many times did it increase? Solar power or wind power are options, but the amount of power consumed goes beyond the reasonable investment limit if it is to be used only for mining - not to mention the extra costs of maintaining such a system, or the renewable energy tax lobby for the oil industry.

Hardware can burn. Graphics cards that are permanently operating at 120% of capacity have a much lower shelf life than the average, and the warranty for the graphics card for an average user is usually 2 years. If the manufacturer expects the graphics card to last approximately 2 years in normal use, how much can it take when it is continuously operating at 120% for over a year? There are also power supply units and other components of such a system - each of them can stop working at any moment.

ASIC

An Application Specific Integrated Circuit (ASIC) is a computer chip created with only one single function in mind. As mining is extremely compute-intensive and requires a lot of resources, some miners decide to devote complete mining machinery to complete machines or parts of machines.

ASIC looks like a Micro PC (pictured above). The device needs electricity and the internet. It does everything on its own - with some settings and optimization, depending on the currency that is being mined and the device itself.

In the beginning, Bitcoin was mined using a simple commercial PC using the power of a processor or graphics card. Today's specialized processors use the so-called ASIC, or inbuilt integrated circuit with a specific purpose, a processor that only performs the task for which it is designed. It takes a certain speed to perform complex calculation operations that graphics cards do not possess to be profitable. Although, they are still used, but only in special configurations called mining rigs or platforms. So, two or more graphics cards are integrated into one whole and perform mining operations.

Cloud Mining

If you have a place with sound insulation and your own power source, you can try to mine in your own space. If you are not able to set up your own mining operation, but you still want to deal with that part of the crypto-world, you can contract with companies dealing exclusively with that service. They have ready-installed computers and are already providing the processor power from them. They do mining operations, and they send you a cryptocurrency to your account for which you have a contract.

The hash, a random and complex combination of numbers and letters, is used to verify transaction blocks in a process known as mining. When the miner calculates the requested hash in the data block, it is rewarded with coins and the percentage of the collected transaction charges that are located within the block, and they are billed to the senders or initiators of the transaction. Calculating hash is a complicated process that often takes several millennia of effort, and success does not necessarily guarantee payment.

Mining is like a competitive sport, and rarely will large players work together. If they work together they must share profit. Unless you own an enormous amount of hashing processor power, and you want to deal with mining, it's a good option to join a mining pool - where you and I can contribute together with a lot of other calculations of these formulas and share success. The rate of calculation is dependent on the hash. With a larger number, the team has a larger number of possible calculations. Hash time is becoming more complicated to prevent inflation and keep rarity of crypts. The following are measures to be used:

KH / s: kilohashes per second, 1000 hashes calculated / s (10^3)

MH / s: Megahashes per second, million hashes calculated/ s (10^6)

GH / s: Gigahashes per second, billions of hashes calculated/ s (10^9)

TH / s: Terrahashes per second, 1 trillion hashes calculated/ s (10^{12})

PH / s: Petahashes per second, 1 quadrillion hashes calculated/ s (10^{15})

Wallets

A cryptocurrency wallet has the same purpose as your typical pocket wallet in that it keeps your digital values. At this point, I must explain that there are two types of miners for two types of currencies: SHA256 and SCRIPT miners. SHA is an abbreviation of Secure Hash Algorithm. Most of the SHA256 include Bitcoin, Bytecoin, Terracoin and the like, and the SCRIPT currencies include the following: Litecoin, Feathercoin, Dogecoin, Sexcoin, Worldcoin and many others. So, if you want to dig BTC, you download the GUIMiner from guiminer.org.

If you want to dig FTC or LTC you can download and install GunnerScript http://guiminer.org/guiminer-scrypt.html. You may also need a program for your Bitcoin ASIC if you have decided to use one. Although some recent models promise that all the settings are already done, including the Bitcoin address; so all you need is to plug it into the power.

The hash rate is the number of billings your equipment can perform every second while trying to solve a mathematical problem. Hash rate is measured in megahash, gigahash and terahash per second (MH / Sec, GH / Sec,and TH / Sec). The higher your hash rate compared to the average hash rate, the more chances you have to resolve the transaction block.

A wallet is a special address that can receive crypts. You can compare it with an email address. The way in which resources are used with the address is to sign a statement (so-called transaction) using a private key (combinations of numbers and letters). The funds in cryptocurrency do not move laterally. The owner of a currency is considered the address that was last published in the blockchain as the owner of that amount of that currency.

The person does not have a coin. 200 others around her say clearly and loudly that she has 500 Bitcoin and they all believe without a doubt. If this person tells all 200 witnesses to give person B of all 500 Bitcoin, all witnesses will confirm this to every new person who enters the circle of these people. So, each newcomer will thus be aware of the fact that person B now has 500 Bitcoin. If a witness says the opposite, the rest will hear and correct him. Blockchain works like this.

Ifa currency exchange is hacked, your assets could be lost. Therefore, if you have an account on a currency exchange, it is recommended that after switching over, transfer funds to an address that is completely under your control.

For example, somebody sends you a virus via email and it usually works by locking files on your computer. Then you are asked to pay a ransom in the battle to send you a program that will unlock your files. This phenomenon has become very widespread and is a major problem.

On the official Bitcoin website just register on the blockchain or Coinbase site (you can choose one of the offered wallets, you have 3 wallet types - Software wallets, Mobile wallets and Web wallets), and, after registration, you get your Bitcoin address. It installs a wallet on your PC, and you can do this by downloading software from Bitcoin.org and installing it on your computer.

The most important component is the graphics card, because the mathematical operations are calculated much faster on a GPU than on a CPU. As I mentioned in an earlier passage, Bitcoin could once have been dug out with a couple of very strong graphics cards, but in time the weight of processing increased so that ordinary graphics cards were not enough to dig. ATI graphics cards series 5, 6 or 7 made about 250 Mhash/s and today are no longer used, because the latest ASIC machines such as KNC Jupiter makes up to 550 GHash/s.

The current price for an ASIC device is too high. Because of this, people usually switch to mining other cryptocurrencies such as Litecoin, Feathercoin, Dogecoin, Sexcoin and Worldcoin. Mining equipment is far cheaper, and these currencies can later be exchanged for Bitcoin. The second most important component in the configuration is a good power supply. Other components are less important. You can take a middle-class computer, but the key components are graphics and power.

Solar mining

Solar mining is a major option for electricity. I wonder what my chances are to run mining equipment using free electricity by hitching a solar panel or a windmill on the roof.

At this time, I see that the prices of the panels and windmills go around $250 for 300W. Is there a chance that I'm going to run some hardware for mining, or will I need at least 5 pieces on the roof?

It takes a lot of money to get started. Major pieces of hardware include deep discharging batteries from several panels, a high-quality converter to 220V (110V in US) and a charger controller.

These solar panels give 300W power at ideal conditions when the sun is very hot. But it needs to accumulate in the battery, and then convert it to 220V in order to start the miner with the converter. 1500W peak power set panels, inverters and batteries could cost $1860. The battery cycle lifetime is 1000 charging / discharging, which means after 1000 cycles (~ 3 years) expect a new investment of $1240 in batteries. So much for a free stream.

Solar panels will cost $3700 for 24/7 mining of one rig. And that's if you buy cheap.
It's best to have two in case one needs to be repaired or have maintenance. Batteries are to be avoided. It would be good if there were an option to pull power from the batteries to supplement times of low power conversion. One solar cell gives 600-700mv in the sun. This is the maximum capacity. You see how much you need the cell?

What do you need for Bitcoin mining? One or more computers with strong graphics cards, preferably AMD Radeon (280X gives a good balance of performance and profitability), or a specialized device that is designed from scratch to maximally solve the Bitcoin algorithm. And that is that! Turn on the gadgets, set up the mining client and the digital wallet location - and the game can start. Actually, it's not fun, but fatiguing, watching the screen and listening to the cooler on the graphics card, which turns like a hungry wolf in January.

The Red Harbinger team launched an Indiegogo campaign to finance the production of the very interesting case they're calling "DopaMINE". The casing is specially designed for users who are seriously mining digital currencies such as Bitcoin, Litecoin or Dogecoin, which specifically requires the support of as many graphics cards as possible. DopaMINE supports up to six graphics cards for maximum GPU performance, while open-air design without side walls should allow for efficient cooling of such configurations. In the lower part of the enclosure, there is a space for two power supplies, while the shape of the carrier is adapted to accommodate more DopaMINE cases by having minimal occupancy space. It is possible to install any motherboards of mini-ITX, micro-

ATX or full ATX format as well as three fans 120 or 140mm in diameter.

Amateur miners may decide to purchase a classic PC configuration with AMD Radeon cards in most cases. Why with Radeon, not with NVIDIA? It's because the Bitcoin algorithm, for some reason, is much faster on AMD than on NVIDIA hardware. There is mining software that is optimized for NVIDIA, but even this is not enough to help NVIDIA cards match the efficiency of the Bitcoin algorithm compared with Radeon. For example, one NVIDIA Titan has performance that is three times less than the twice cheaper Radeon 290, making them five to six times more cost effective. "AMD Radeon all the way," advises the ScreenFun magazine.

Is it worth it?

Is mining worthwhile, since everyone is talking about it and more and more people are moving to buy equipment? At the current value of Bitcoin, an investment of $10,000 in equipment would return in seven or eight months. Of course, due to the very nature of this currency, drastic drops and drastic jumps are possible. So it is not excluded that the new investor will burst like a pumpkin, but could also earn double. Market disruptions, such as the recent bankruptcy of Mt. Gox, Bitcoin's exchange office in Tokyo, have a negative impact on people's confidence in Bitcoin and other crypts, and there is a legal regulation that some countries, such as China and Russia, that try to limit or ban the purchase and sale of goods and services with cryptocurrency.

AMD/ATI graphics have long been the only logical choice for Bitcoin mining due to far superior GPGP performance compared to NVIDIA; they have a much higher performance, especially since NVIDIA has saturated its own OpenCL performance with the introduction of the GTX6xx series.

CHAPTER THREE
CRYPTO COINS

Bitcoin

As a cryptographic currency, BTC is not recognized by any country. There is no institution and no individual business entity representing it. It is a program that is constantly running on the internet, supported by thousands of computers that handle transactions that direct the BTC between users. It also keeps track of the amount found in your digital wallet (which you hold in your phone, on your computer's hard drive, on a USB drive, or on the internet).

A digital, virtual Bitcoin wallet is also a place to store Bitcoin. It works like any account you can open at the bank. The advantages that such an account has over others is that it's simple and safe. Since Bitcoin, as a pay-per-use tool that is mostly used on the internet, takes on more and more of online payments, it's wise to own one.

The mining industry of Bitcoin consumes 22.5 terawatt-hours(TWh) per hour per year. It's the equivalent of 13.24 million barrels of oil. Since 12.5 Bitcoins are being exploited every 10 minutes, the average power consumption per bit is equal to 20 barrels of oil equivalent. Bitcoin mining has the potential to be a rather profitable business, given that one Bitcoin is now worth more than 100 barrels of oil.

You are well equipped and ready for the patience that Bitcoin's mining requires, these are the steps you should take:

Get your wallet. This is something like a PayPal account, where you can keep your Bitcoins. The Wallet may be online or on your computer, and for installation, you will need to download a large blockchain file. One of the most popular platforms for wallets is Coinbase.

Pools are networks of computers that are bound to the common mining in order to convert complex mathematical operations as soon as possible into electronic money. The first, and still one of the most valuable packs, is Slush's Pool, but keep in mind that each pool takes a commission to use the services (usually one Bitcoin block contains 25 units of currency).

Install Bitcoin Miner on your computer. This is software that solves the aforementioned mathematical operations to reach Bitcoin. We won't go too deep with technical information. Instead, we will only mention two types, CPUs and GPUs, and beginners are recommended Kivy's GUI.

Create and log into your account on PulseWallet and enter the address of your wallet. Here you will find the wallet itself. Register your workers. This is a revolutionary biometric digital wallet. Its software tracks the work of your miners and tells you how the mining of the device is progressing. It also alerts you to whether there was a problem somewhere, like warming up the computer and the like. It registers as sub-accounts of your basic order. Enter your employee information in the mining software, and then enter the URL of your pool, and mining can start.

One thing Bitcoin has in common with gold, is that the precious metal has limited quantities. Only 21,000,000 Bitcoin will ever exist,and nearly everyone will dig this up by the year 2140. The more it is dug up, the harder it will be to find. Bitcoin actually works a little differently and is quite ingenious when you figure it out. One of the main differences is that mining does not necessarily create Bitcoin. Bitcoin is awarded as a prize for verifying previous transactions. So how is this done? Bitcoin mining requires a computer and a specialized program. Miners, using the program and a large number of computer resources, solve complicated mathematical problems. Every 10 minutes, miners have the opportunity to solve a block containing the most recent transaction data using a cryptographic hash function.

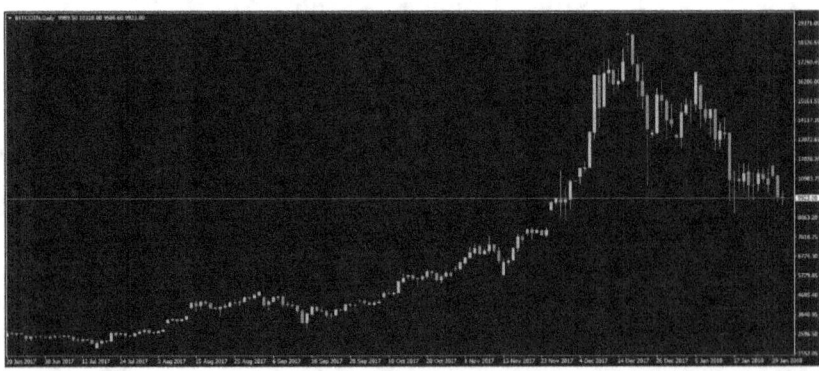

Bitcoin miners are running in search of an input that gives a specific value (a number with more zeros at the beginning). The weight of these riddles can be measured. It is impossible to fool them. The goal of mining is to use a computer to negotiate until it hits a good value less than what is targeted. If you are the first to do this, it means you have dug up the block (normally, millions of computers around the world are generating their hits). Whoever digs the block as a reward gets 12.5 Bitcoin (as long as it's part of the long block). The winner does not technically create Bitcoin, but the encoding of the block algorithm is set to reward the miner and thus help the blocking verification. Each block is created in sequences, including the preceding block. Because each block contains something from the previous one, this proves that it came after it. Sometimes, two competitors on the block form different minerals. They may contain different Bitcoin transactions initiated from different locations.

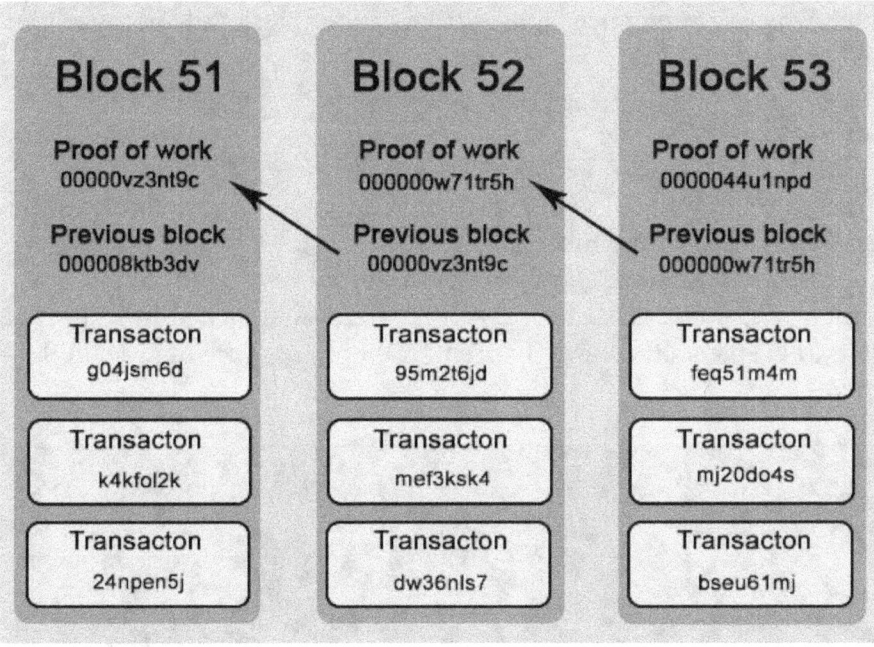

Classic mining is when a user uses his computer, specifically a Bitcoin mining graphic map. Lately, classical mining of Bitcoin has become absolutely unprofitable and is not worth trying. This is because the hardware that is needed is very expensive, and the weight of the mining and consumed electricity is too big. There is too much overhead, so there is no profit. For mining, you need a specialized computer, a rig that is similar to a regular computer, but it has a built-in high-end graphics card and that consumes considerably more current than your regular computer.

So, the rig is embedded with: a motherboard that has multiple PCIe slots and thus supports the installation of multiple graphics cards, processor, RAM, stronger and a high-quality power supply (800W, 1000W of a brand of manufacturers such as cooler master). The most important part of graphic map mining is cables for connecting a graphics on a board (raster) and, of course, an internet connection. In the rigs for mining, mainly graphics cards of higher classes are used to achieve greater power. From the beginning, chips made by AMD (formerly ATI) have a great advantage for mining. At the moment of writing this text, the cheapest graphical maps for mining are the AMD RX460 or RX560, but of course, you need multiples of them. It is recommended to use stronger graphics cards because they have a higher power.

Ethereum

Minergate's main goal is to make mining available to amateurs. The variable weight of the mining is adapted to the power of the processor and the user's graphics card. It makes it possible for mining with weaker hardware. Minergate was launched in 2014 by a team of crypto-enthusiasts. Currently, there are more than 100,000 active users.

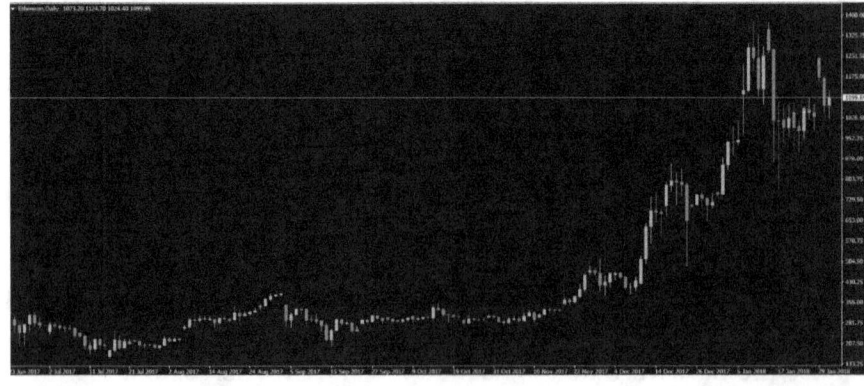

Advantages and disadvantages of mining of Ethereum

Independent and pool miners have mined Ethereum since the first block (07/30/15). The growing popularity of Ethereum reached its peak in March 2016, when its total market value exceeded one billion dollars. Not surprisingly, a large number of people want to join and gain a share of the profits; the total power of the Ethereum network is estimated at around 2.4 TH / s, with most of that power being deployed from several of the strongest mining pools.

The popularity of this crypto makes mining senseless for amateurs. The GeForce GTX 960, one of the most popular graphics cards, would have to mine Ethereum about 5 months before it paid for itself. It is expected that the weight of the mining industry will continue to grow.

This means that people will gradually switch to mining pools. It will allow their members to pool resources and thus have a more predictable profit than in the case of the miners themselves. For this reason, Minergate's GUI Miner is one of the simplest to use; with one click you start the process. The owners of the pools were guided by the same principles during the implementation of the Ethereum mining.

Claude Lecomte, the director of Minergate, comments on the mining industry and the new options offered by Minergate. According to Lecomte, Minergate has a 1-click GUI Miner that allows people to easily enter the world of mining. Minergate software does not require system configuration or study of tutorials. The user only installs the application and clicks on start mining. This is very important because many users do not have the technical knowledge but do have the relatively strong hardware. When it comes to Ethereum, it's mostly mined by gamers with strong graphics cards.

Lecomte believes that Ethereum is one of the most advanced technologies of today. He also thinks that the secret of its success is that it is not positioned as a modern crypto. It is a blockchain platform that allows creating a new value by creating applications on that platform.

Now that Minergate added Ethereum to their 1-click GUI miner it's possible to begin mining in just a few seconds and earning from mining on ordinary computers.

When it comes to the mining pools, it is also commonly said that the very concept is completely contrary to the original crypto-philosophy of decentralization. It combines strength in the pulse, centralizing power and endangering network security. It believes that market laws help reduce this risk by increasing demand that results in a better supply on the market.

Litecoin

Usually, the Altcoin Mining uses the 3xRadeon R9 290x as well as the motherboard ASRock or SNIPER. The price of the Litecoin mining machine is far cheaper than the one for Bitcoin. It is currently the most cost-effective investment.

This currency could be digested with ordinary computers with graphics cards. It could not work with ASIC mines for Bitcoin. It is based on a script algorithm that enables digging with graphics cards. ATI cards, especially the R9 series are currently valid as the fastest.

Litecoin was a fertile soil for the creation of many other crypts, most of which were mostly copies of it. These currencies now have hundreds, but Litecoin remains the most popular. They are speculating that ASIC miners for Litecoin (and consequently all its clones) are now made, which will potentially decrease the efficacy of using Litecoin inject video cards.

Monero

Monero is the only currency that can be mined with processors and graphics cards. I work with both together. The most profitable graphics for Monero is either VEGA 56 or 64,which gives you 2000h / s. The Ryzen 7 1700 gives you about 600h / s. The fx8350 gives 400h / s (older processor about 240km) and the rx580 about 750 h / s.

Monero uses the Crypto Night algorithm, and as you see the site listed below, you are already proposing some high hash rates compared with the price of electricity and consumption. Enter 2000h / s 200w and calculate how much you return monthly.

Another important thing about Monero is the amount of newly-made Monero coins is proportionally decreasing every day. It will take a long time for the price to increase. In 1 year it is halved. While for Bitcoin it is every 4 years. Block size is changeable. Bitcoin is 1MB fixed (because now the transaction is 24h late in Bitcoin).

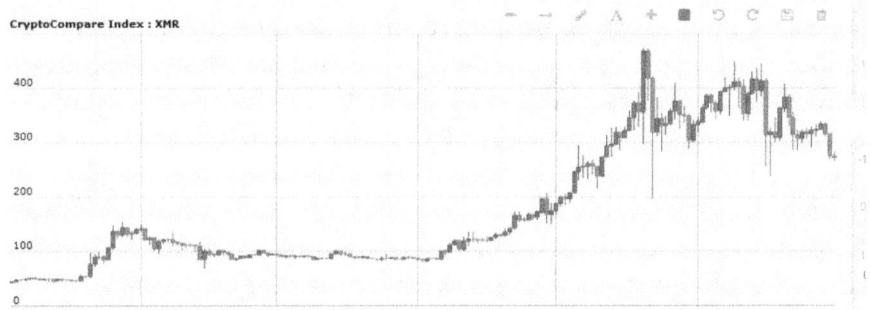

https://www.cryptocompare.com/coins/xmr/charts/USD?p=6M

Ubiq

The specialty of this crypto is writing smart contracts in Solidity language and creating dApps (decentralized applications) on its blockchain. What distinguishes it from Ethereum is that it offers business users and startups a stable and secure option to use a blockchain.

The platform was created by cleavage of the code (English fork) of Ethereum. It is not illegal or prohibited (it is even encouraged by the decentralization of the entire system) since it is not possible to implement a new version of the code in the former version of the protocol.

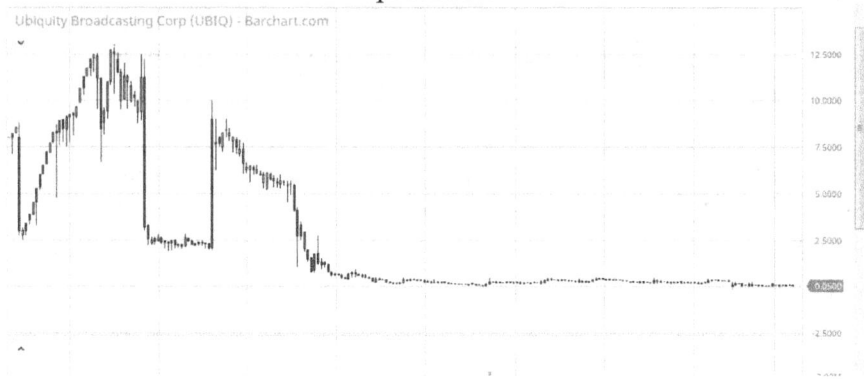

https://www.barchart.com/stocks/quotes/UBIQ/interactive-chart

Very soon after its creation (October 23, 2014), Coinmarketscoin became Jumbucks crypt. Jumbucks was based on the Proof of Stake consensus and in very short time received community support. Various developers then contributed to their ideas, improved the platform at that time, and gave meaning to the decentralization of the entire system.

As such, it existed until January 28, 2017, the year when Ubiq was founded, which functions on the Proof of Work consensus. The problem is obvious; too many links have resulted in less stability and security. Also, switching to the PoW system has enabled a wider audience the opportunity to mine instead of investing in the amount of currency held (their stake). Anyone who owned the Jumbucks crypto could be replaced by a ratio of 1:10. With the creation of Ubiq, there was a transition to the Ethereum protocol, which was not the case with Coinmarketscoin and Jumbucks.

There is good reason for switching to Ethereum's upgraded protocol. The very protocol on which dApp is based can be modified with the agreement of most miners, or those who have a "stake" (PoS). But then that token is in danger of collapse, because eventually everything depends on one computer. Of course, here we take into account this will not be the case with all crypts, some tokens can't be mined.

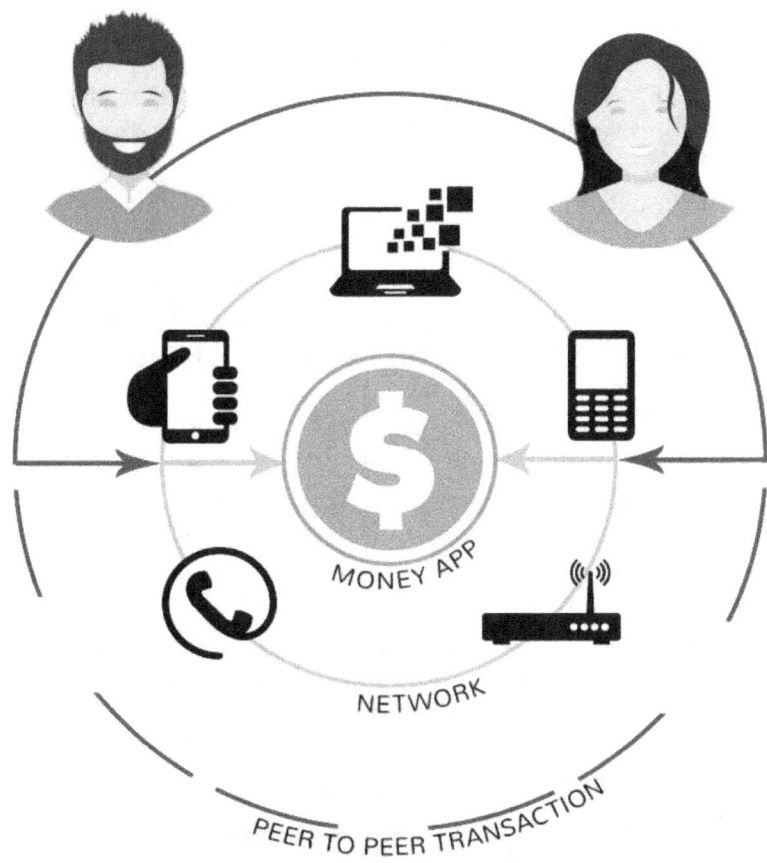

Ubiq cryptocurrency has a developed monetary policy. It ensures that miners are paid very little, and therefore the interest in mining was so small.that the developed algorithm did not adjust the weight of the cryptographic task to obtain an average. The crypto-proof was created without an ICO, which means it's not beyond the legal framework (remember China stopped the ICO). It was also not mined before the market offer, which is actually a relatively common practice. Nonetheless, a large number of development teams mine their cryptocurrency before offering on the market to create quick profits. The development team, like all the others who are interested in owning Ubiq, must mine the crypto or buy it on the stock exchanges that offer it: Bittrex, Cryptopia, LiteBit.

Hard Forks of Bitcoin

There will be a split in the market.In the same way Bitcoin Cash appeared, a new crypto will appear. There is also some nervousness in the market, because the public is not aware of what it actually means; the volume of Bitcoin coins will not increase the same as it did after Bitcoin Cash appeared.

What are the consequences for the "real" Bitcoin?

There is only one Bitcoin and there will only be one Bitcoin. Therefore, 21 million coins will remain in circulation, which can be purchased under the name Bitcoin. Bitcoin Gold, together with Bitcoin Cash, represent a new currency, just like Litecoin, Dash and other crypts. After breaking into Bitcoin Gold, all owners and investors who own Bitcoin will receive the same amount of Bitcoin Gold coins in their hands. Having received Bitcoin Gold coins in their wallets, investors can work with them in any way they want from selling to storing in a wallet.

Bitcoin Cash and Bitcoin Gold by no means register on the Bitcoin network, but Bitcoin owners get them and thus profit more than owners who hold other crypts.

One of the options is Zcash. You will ask yourself "is this just another of many altogether?" In short, yes, only with a variation of a higher degree of privacy.

Zcash

The Zcash model is similar to Bitcoin. Everything is still open-source. The final number of coins in circulation is 21 million. However, the distribution model is different. 10% of the total quantity will be distributed among founders, investors, employees,and advisers. The company believes it will motivate founders to support Zcash in the long run, reducing the possibility of a "pump-and-dump" action.

The founders have reached a mutual agreement that 1% of the total amount will be awarded by the non-profit Zcash Foundation. The Foundation is in charge of maintaining and developing protocols and software.

The main difference between Bitcoin and Zcash is already mentioned - privacy. While addresses and transfer values are available to the public, Zcash also encrypts this information by default, and only the person who created the transaction can make the information public.

Another difference is the method of mining and the way in which full nodes confirm the validity of the transactions. The algorithm is called zero-knowledge proofs. In short, the transaction maker includes proof of validity that it is not double spent, without detecting encrypted data. Vilcox estimates that the first real block will be in July of this year (2018). He wants the mining to be available to as many people as possible, and therefore try to enable the use of Zcash on mobile devices.

CHAPTER FOUR
BITCOIN SCAMS

Bitcoin scams

There are more and more reports pointing the finger at North Korea as the place where most hacker attacks come to the crypto market. Following the accusation that the most mysterious country in the world is responsible for WannaCry malware, new evidence is coming out. The Recorded Future Internet Security Company claims in its report that the new attacks are very similar to the 2014 attack on Sony Pictures. An investigation by Recorded Future found that after the attacks on the exchange, crypts were exchanged in South Korea. The report links this activity to the hacker group Lazarus, which is connected to North Korea. The malware for the attack was created mid-late last year, at a time when Bitcoin, as well as another crypto, began to jump.

According to Recorded Future, this is all part of a broad campaign by North Korea's, which is very interested in cryptography. This interest involves the mining, software and theft of crypts. The report does not say how these attackers are successful in their campaigns of the collection of personal data of users involved with cryptocurrency exchange. Previous reports of security companies, as well as South Korea's state institutions, say North Korea's hackers are responsible for the crippled exchange crises last summer. North Korea has so far denied all accusations, but it also does not hide its interest in Bitcoin and other crypts. Frequent attacks on crypto-exchange sites come at a time when South Korea is considering the possibility of banning crypto-trades. If that happens, hackers will focus their attention on wallets on servers outside the Asian continent.

This news, along with the announcement that China is considering a crypto-prohibition, has led to a sharp fall in crypts that lost 20% of their value in one day. Bitcoin is currently worth a little over $10,000, and not so long ago, it crossed the limit of $20,000. If you hold dozens of coins, we hope you will have luck and patience. If it's any consolation, it's believed that this is just an immediate fall in value, unless the hackers continue to steal. South Korean minister Kim Dong-Jeon told a local radio station that the Seoul government would soon come up with measures to combat the irrational investment-related cyber-insanity.

This news broke the value of Bitcoin, which is traded on the Luxembourg Stock Exchange Bitstamp at a price of $11,730. That's a 13.6 percent drop in one day.

Since mid-December 2017, when it reached a record value of $20,000, Bitcoin has dropped more than 40 percent. Hence its market capitalization has been reduced by 125 billion dollars. The value of other digital currencies fell, with Ethereum sliding 7.8 percent to $1,190.

China allowed Bitcoin to own and trade through physical, but not legal entities, including financial institutions such as banks. On December 5, 2013, the National Bank of China, put into effect the aforementioned prohibition on companies managing Bitcoin transactions, regulating the status of this currency for the first time. After this decision, all Bitcoin accounts in Chinese commercial banks had to be closed by mid-April 2014.

Since the beginning of the year, it is public knowledge that the National Bank of China is intensely preparing detailed regulation in the area of digital currencies since 50% of the value of Bitcoin is located in this country. The relationship of new Chinese regulations to Bitcoin will greatly affect its future value and the natureof other legislation to the new currency. The decision by the Chinese government to "temporarily" prohibit the purchase and sale of ICO tokens, reflected the value of all the currencies, and they lost half their value in a short period, as China was expected to follow other countries. However, with the exception of South Korea, the chain reaction ban was avoided, so the crypts recovered and continued to grow to record values by the end of the year.

There are free services offered that guarantee that "in only a few minutes/hours you will earn multiple times Bitcoin than you have invested." Apparently, this is possible because there are flaws in Bitcoin clients and transactions. Why do they not charge for the service? Because they believe in technology and its progress.

Just read the previous paragraph and realize that it is another scam that uses the technique of social manipulation. Today, at its address, mtgox.com opens to a completely blank page, which means that millions of user deposits around the world have vanished. The MtGox Twitter account was also completely cleaned, and other major players from the Bitcoin sphere announced that the wheat is being separated from the chaff. This caused sufficient panic to drop BTC by 20 percent.

A document, the authenticity of which has not been confirmed, is being circulated on the internet. It alleges the crisis strategy of MtGox and mentions the theft of as much as 750,000 Bitcoin (the current value of about $380 million), which has been hiding from the public for nearly three years. The document also recalls that Mark Karpeles, executive director of the company, resigned on Sunday in the boardroom of the BitCoinFoundation, which promotes the cryptocurrency. The alleged crisis document contains claims that a huge loss was recorded in 2011, and that it was the result of the same transaction problem which forced the company to block the withdrawal of BTC earlier in the month.

It also states that a crisis strategy was proposed by Gox.com, claiming that losses should be compensated by donations of big players in the battlefields, which would not be worth anything with the collapse of the currency. At the same time, an open letter was signed by several leading people of the online stock exchanges for crypts, stating that MtGox in private conversations confirmed the existence of certain problems.

Just like in every new industry, there is a crop that needs to be separated from the grain, that's what we see at work now. We are confident that strong Bitcoin companies, run by teams of capable people and supported by credible investors, will continue to strengthen and fulfill the promise that will be the future of transactions in the internet era.

Of course, this event occurred when the currency was at its then peak, exchanging for a sum of more than $1,000. After a fall of 22 percent, Bitcoin dropped even more from $581 to $437. Throughout the internet, confessions of many yesterday's millionaires can be found, whose deposits were trapped in the newly emerging "white" MtGox. MtGox is a Japanese company that started trading as a card trading company from the popular Magic the Gathering game, but in 2010 it turned to Bitcoin. Under new leadership in 2013 it performed as much as 70 percent of global transactions in this currency.

Conclusion

This book presented four chapters: basiccryptocurrency, mining, crypto coins and Bitcoin scams. In the first chapter it detailed what cryptocurrency is and how the blockchain works.

The second chapter explained types of mining, which includes cloud mining and rig mining. Rig mining is divided into pool, or group, mining and solo mining. It requires a powerful computer to mine. The pool takes 1% profit for itself. Electricity costs can raise. Graphics cards are operated at 120% of capacity. A detailed breakdown of costs was presented. Solar mining dependson electricity. Solar panels cost $250.

The third chapter gave a deep analysis of crypto coins. They are Bitcoin, Ethereum. Litecoin, Monero,and Ubiq. Bitcoin reached over $20,000 in December. It is now trading below$10,000. As of the publication of this book it has lost almost 50% retained gain in the last month. Ethereum peaked at $1400. It also fell and is now trading at $1000. Litecoin was trading at its highest at $365 while it was trading below $150 as of yesterday. Monero is now trading at $245. Its highest price was $474. Ubiq was trading above $0.05 while the highest price was $12.50. All coins are trading at the platforms exchange.

The last chapter explained scams in cryptocurrency. Bitcoin and cryptocurrencies faced a decline in value. It is speculated this has much to do with the decision of South Korea. In the meantime, several traders of cryptocurrency in Seoul are now under investigation for alleged tax evasion. In this country, few people own and trade crypts, wild price changes have become an everyday occurence, and way too much attention is given to this price fluctuation. There is great concern about virtual currencies, and the Justice Ministry is preparing for a ban on crypto-trading. Out of South Korea came an attack on one of the largest stock exchanges for the sale and purchase of Bitcoin, the South Korean stock exchange Bithumb. The government of South Korea previously announced that it will use more oversight over exchanges, including moves to abolish anonymous trade. Bitcoin experienced a collapse and fell to $13,000 at a CoinDesk price index after reports that South Korea plans to ban all types of trade and exchange using crypts.

The Bitcoin mining platform NiceHash was hacked in Slovenia, and it is suspected that tens of millions of dollars were stolen. The NiceHash platform is conducting a security breach investigation and will suspend business for 24 hours until it determines how much was stolen. Research firm Coindesk says about 4700 Bitcoins were stolen, worth nearly $66 million, as the crypt has reached a recorded price of $14,000.

It was a hacker attack. It became clear after some Bithumb customers reported that their money had disappeared from their accounts. The South Korean Internet and Security Agency was also involved in the investigation, but according to currently available information, user passwords were not stolen, only money.

It was a personal computer of one of the employees that was hacked, not the main server. Any personal information from customers, such as mobile phone numbers and e-mail addresses, were not discovered. Hackers were only given access to one-time passwords used in electronic financial transactions. Although not officially confirmed, it is an alleged theft of several billion won or several million dollars.

Bithumb is one of the largest and busiest Bitcoin exchanges in the world, and this case only shows that the jump in crypto-values has sparked the attention not only of buyers and sellers but also of hackers. After all, this is not the first case of the "disappearance" of large quantities of crypts. In 2014 another stock market - Mt. Gox - was destroyed in a hacking attack. At that time, $460 million worth of bits were lost. Bitcoin was worth much less than today. With the rise in crypto-values and an increasing number of users, it is expected that such cases will be repeated more and more frequently.

Thank you for purchasing and reading this book, *Cryptocurrency King: From Beginner to Expert*. You are now well educated on the ins and outs of the industry. You have the basic knowledge to begin interacting in the world of cryptocurrency. Though the industry has been going through some growing pains, I'm confident that the future of cryptocurrency is bright.

There has never been a better time to get involved in this young, game-changing currency model! Good luck!

www.ingramcontent.com/pod-product-compliance
Lightning Source LLC
Chambersburg PA
CBHW030103230526
45471CB00003B/1228